A QUANTUM BOOK

Published by
Chartwell Books
A Division of Book Sales, Inc.
114 Northfield Avenue
Edison, New Jersey, 08837
USA

ISBN 0-7858-0678-4

This book was produced by
Quantum Books Ltd
6 Blundell Street
London N7 9BH

Produced in Australia by Griffin Colour

Candy MAKING
Hilary Walden

CHARTWELL
BOOKS, INC.

F·U·D·G·E

The sugar syrup for fudge is boiled to the soft ball stage and is then beaten to encourage crystalization of the sugar and give the fudge its characteristic texture and appearance. These can, in fact, be changed slightly by beating the syrup at different times – immediately after it has been cooked or after it has been left to cool. Firmer sweets with a more granular texture will result from beating in hot syrup while smooth fudge is the outcome of leaving the syrup to cool.

Stir fudge mixtures with a high milk or cream content to prevent them sticking and burning, and be sure to use a large enough saucepan as they will boil up considerably.

1 Place the thermometer in hot water to warm it. Oil the pan.

2 Gently heat the sugar with the milk, cream or diced butter and any other ingredients according to the recipe, in a thick saucepan that has a capacity at least four times the volume of the ingredients, stirring with a wooden spoon until the sugar has dissolved and any butter or chocolate melted.

3 Bring to a boil, cover and boil for about 3 minutes.

4 Uncover and boil until the required temperature has been reached, stirring as necessary if the mixture has a high milk or cream content.

5 Dip the pan in cold water.

6 Either beat the mixture immediately with a wooden spoon until it begins to thicken and becomes lighter in color and loses its gloss, then quickly pour into the pan and leave until beginning to set. Or, leave the mixture to cool to about 122°F and starting to become opaque, then beat until it becomes paler and thickens (below).

7 Pour into the pan and leave to set.

8 Mark into squares and allow to set completely.

9 Break into pieces and store in an airtight container between layers of waxed paper.

F·O·N·D·A·N·T

Fondant consists essentially of a mass of minute sugar crystals surrounded by a saturated sugar syrup. The creamy, smooth, melting texture is achieved through a series of precise stages, the first of which is the addition of glucose to the syrup to make sure that the sugar crystals formed during the later stages remain small so keeping the fondant smooth (glucose keeps the fondant softer for longer than would cream of tartar or another acid). The next stage is when the hot syrup is poured into a pool and the edges folded inwards to cool it quickly and evenly before it is 'worked' to develop the crystalization of the sugar. To free it of lumps the fondant is kneaded, like a dough for bread. It must then be left for at least 12 hours for the sugar crystals to undergo their final change, softening the fondant.

---

1 Sprinkle an even coating of cold water over a marble slab or other suitable work surface.

2 Prepare a sugar, incorporating glucose, to 240°F, the soft ball stage.

3 Dip the saucepan in cold water then quickly pour the syrup into a pool onto the surface and allow to cool for a few minutes.

4 Using a dampened metal spatula or large metal palette knife, lift the edges of the pool of syrup and fold them to the center. Repeat until the syrup becomes glossy and viscous and has a faint yellow color (below).

5 Using a dampened wooden spatula work the mixture in a continuous figure of eight action for 5–10 minutes.

6 Stir until it becomes white and crumbly and the stirring is extremely difficult.

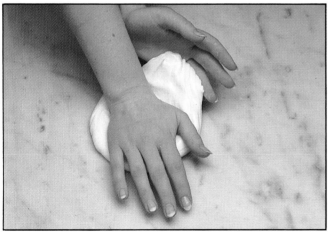

7 With lightly moistened hands, form a ball of fondant then knead it by pushing half of the ball away from you with the heel of one hand, fold the half back into the lump using a metal spatula or palette knife and repeat in a flowing action for 5–10 minutes until the mixture is free of lumps and feels smooth.

8 Form the fondant into a ball, place it on a dampened plate, cover with a damp cloth to prevent the surface drying out and leave in a cool place for at least 12 hours.

1 Fruits have have a stem or stalk – hold the fruit by the stem or stalk then dip it into the melted fondant so that it is about three-quarters coated.

2 Lift it out, allowing the excess to drain off and dip in sugar.

3 Leave the fruit on waxed paper to dry.

4 Portions of fruit without stems – place the fruit on a dipping fork and lower it into the melted fondant. Turn it over so that it is completely covered.

5 Lift the fruit out on the dipping fork, tap the fork lightly on the side of the bowl then draw the bottom of the fork across the edge of the bowl. Carefully transfer the fruit to waxed paper and allow to dry.

C·A·R·A·M·E·L·S

The traditional mellow, soft, creamy flavor of caramel sweets is obtained by the addition of milk, or milk products such as cream, evaporated or condensed milk, and butter, and not, as the name suggests, by caramelizing the sugar. The characteristic chewy, moist texture comes from boiling the syrup as far as the firm ball stage, 244–250°F. However, the degree of firmness can be varied by taking the syrup to different points within the firm-hard ball range – the nearer to the top of the range, the firmer the sweet.

It is especially important when making caramels to use a sufficiently large saucepan because the mixture expands considerably as it boils. Because of their milk, cream or butter content, caramels are liable to stick to the saucepan and therefore burn, so stirring becomes a necessity. Their thickening effect on the syrup provides some protection against crystalization of the sugar, but for a complete safeguard another anti-crystalizing agent is usually added as well.

1 Line the base of a pan with a piece of oiled waxed paper.

2 Gently heat the sugar with the milk, cream or diced butter and anti-crystalizing agent in a heavy saucepan that has a capacity at least four times the volume of the ingredients.

3 Stir with a wooden spoon until the sugar has dissolved and any butter melted.

4 Bring to a boil, cover and boil for about 3 minutes.

5 Put the warmed thermometer in place and boil, stirring gently occasionally and taking care not to knock the thermometer, until the syrup reaches the required temperature.

6 Dip the saucepan in cold water to prevent the temperature rising further, then pour the caramel into the pan.

7 Allow to cool. Mark it into pieces when just beginning to set and before it becomes too hard. Oiling the knife will prevent sticking.

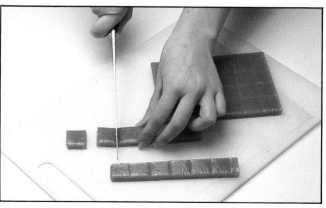

8 When the caramel is completely cold and firm, turn it out of the pan, remove the paper and divide it into the marked pieces. Wrap the caramel pieces in cellophane or waxed paper.

M·A·R·S·H·M·A·L·L·O·W·S

The basis for marshmallows is a syrup boiled to the hard ball stage, 250–266°F. Gelatin and stiffly beaten egg white are incorporated to transform it into softly set airy clouds.

The syrup with the dissolved gelatin must be poured into the egg whites in a slow, thin, steady stream, and the whites must be whisked constantly otherwise the weight of the syrup will knock the air bubbles out of them. A food mixer is therefore a great boon, but failing that, place the bowl containing the egg whites on a damp cloth to hold it steady. Whisking must continue until the mixture is very fluffy and light before it can be left to set. For this, an oiled pan well dusted with a mixture of sifted cornstarch and confectioner's sugar is used. All the surfaces of marshmallows are coated in cornstarch/confectioner's sugar to prevent them sticking together.

1 Prepare the pan.

2 Boil a syrup to hard ball stage.

3 Meanwhile, mix the gelatin with a little cold water in a small bowl, place the bowl in a larger bowl of hot water and heat until dissolved.

4 Whisk the egg whites with a wire whisk (this gives a greater volume than a rotary or electric whisk) until stiff peaks are formed.

5 Add the gelatin to the syrup.

6 Then pour the syrup into the egg whites in a slow, thin, steady stream down the sides of the bowl.

7 Continue to whisk the mixture until it is very fluffy and light and just holds its shape firmly but is still thin enough to turn into the pan without difficulty. This may take 15–20 minutes.

8 Turn the mixture into the pan, lightly smoothing it out evenly and leveling the surface with a metal palette knife. Leave to set.

9 Sift an even coating of cornstarch mixed with confectioner's sugar onto the work surface. Loosen around the sides of the pan containing the marshmallow with a small knife then invert the marshmallow onto the prepared surface.

10 Lightly coat the top and sides with cornstarch/confectioner's sugar. Cut into pieces using a large, oiled knife or sharp scissors or oiled metal cutters.

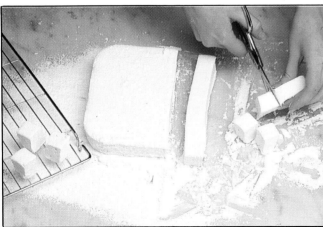

11 Coat the sides of the pieces with cornstarch/confectioner's sugar, then place on a wire rack to dry.

N·O·U·G·A·T

There are two cooking processes involved in the preparation of nougat. The first is the boiling of the sugar syrup to the soft crack stage, 280°F: the second, a much more gentle one, 'sets' the stiffly beaten egg whites that have been added. As soon as the mixture thickens, it must be removed from the heat to avoid overcooking. To achieve the unique, compact chewy texture, one more, very simple step is necessary – the mixture must be weighted down overnight.

The nuts that are included in nearly every nougat recipe must be warmed slightly otherwise they will cause, premature, localized setting. Honey, another traditional ingredient in many nougat recipes, is added to the syrup near the end of its preparation, as its characteristic flavor is changed by cooking.

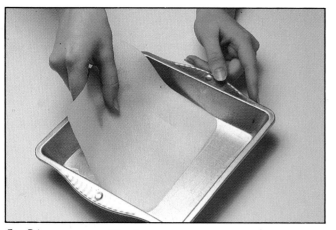

1 Line a pan with rice paper.

2 Melt the honey in a bowl placed over a saucepan of hot water.

3 Prepare a sugar syrup containing glucose to the soft crack stage.

4 Pour the honey into the syrup and boil to 290°F.

5 Dip the pan in cold water.

6 Whisk the egg whites stiffly then pour the syrup into them in a slow, thin, steady stream, whisking constantly.

7 Place the bowl over a pan of just summering water and whisk until the mixture becomes firm.

8 Remove from the heat, stir in the warmed nuts, cherries and angelica.

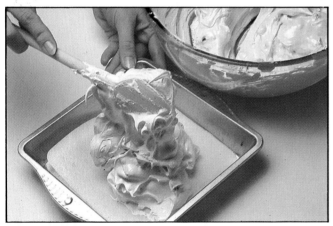

9 Pour into the pan and spread out evenly.

11 Turn the nougat out of the pan, trim away excess rice paper and cut the nougat into squares or fingers using a large sharp knife. Wrap in cellophane and store in an airtight container.

10 Cover with rice paper, place a board on top and place weights on the board. Allow to set overnight.

CHOCOLATE WORK

The chocolate for 'chocolates' should be the best that you can buy. It is just not worth spending the time to make sweets from cheap brands of chocolate, cheap 'cooking' chocolate sold in unlabeled bags, or chocolate-flavored cake coverings. Special 'dipping' chocolate is available from good confectioners, or use a good quality dessert chocolate. For the most 'chocolatey' flavor use the least sweetened or bitter variety of dark chocolate.

• MELTING CHOCOLATE •

It is vital that the chocolate is melted with care, so don't rush it.

1 Chop the chocolate so that it will melt more quickly and evenly. Put it into a bowl placed over a saucepan of hot but not boiling water, making sure that the bottom of the bowl does not touch the water. (A heat-resistant glass bowl will enable you to check easily whether the water is bubbling and whether the bottom of the bowl is clear of the water.)

2 Remove the saucepan from the heat and stir the chocolate occasionally as it softens until it is free of lumps. Then stir it until it is smooth and liquid. Do not allow the temperature to rise higher than 120°F otherwise the flavor of the chocolate will be spoilt.

3 Leave the chocolate to cool and therefore thicken slightly before using it. Once the right coating consistency is reached, keep the temperature constant by putting the bowl over hot water or removing it, as necessary. Throughout the process make sure that no steam or drop of water gets into the chocolate as it will spoil the gloss of the sweets.

It is especially important when working with chocolate to remember that it will not adhere to a wet or sticky surface, so make sure that any mold to be lined or any ingredient to be coated is completely dry – make caramels, fondants, and marzipans a day in advance to give the outside a chance to dry out.

1 Melt the chocolate. Place one center at a time in the chocolate, turn it over gently with a fork then lift it out on the prongs.

2 Tap the fork on the rim of the bowl then draw the underside of the fork over the rim to remove any drips of chocolate.

3 Gently put the sweet onto a tray lined with waxed paper and allow to dry.

4 Repeat with the remaining centers, keeping a check on the temperature of the chocolate to make sure that it does not become too hot.

• DECORATING CHOCOLATES •

This must be done while the chocolate is still wet.

• SIMPLE RIDGE •

Place the end of a round-bladed knife on top of the chocolate, then lightly draw it over the surface to leave a ridge of chocolate.

• A SERIES OF PARALLEL LINES •

Place the back of the prongs of a fork flat on the chocolate, then raise the fork straight upwards slightly, taking with it threads of chocolate to form ridges. Then carefully draw the fork straight backwards towards you.

• A CIRCLE ON A ROUND SHAPE •

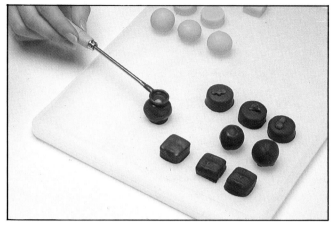

Place a round dipping fork – or similar circular shape such as the end of a long kebab skewer – on the surface of the chocolate. Raise it straight upwards slightly, taking threads of chocolate with it to form a ridge, then carefully draw the fork or skewer straight backwards towards you.

• PIPING •

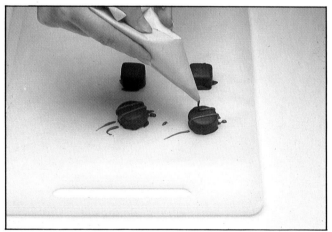

Fill a waxed paper piping bag with melted chocolate of a contrasting color to the sweet, snip off the end of the bag then pipe fine lines over the surface of the sweet.

EASY LIQUEUR OR COCKTAIL CHOCOLATES

· EASY LIQUEUR OR COCKTAIL CHOCOLATES ·

1 Spoon a little melted chocolate into small foil chocolate cases, then gently tip and rotate the case to coat the sides evenly with chocolate. Pour any excess chocolate back into the bulk of the chocolate. Allow the cases to set.

2 Drop small blobs of chocolate on waxed paper equal to the number of cases. Spread the blobs out to small circles to fit the tops of the cases. Allow to set.

3 Fill the cases with the chosen spirit, liqueur or cocktail based on a spirit or liqueur.

4 Carefully lift the chocolate circles from the waxed paper.

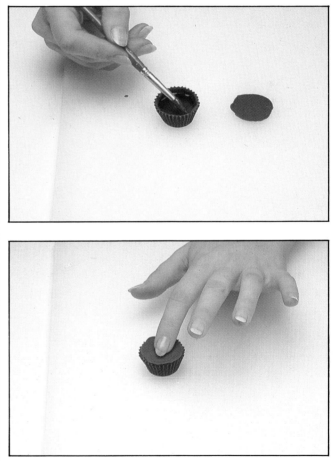

5 To fix the lids, use a fine artist's or make-up brush, point of a sharp knife, or piping bag. Run a little melted chocolate around the edge of the cases, then press the lids lightly in place and put aside to set.

1 Melt some chocolate – the amount will depend on the size of the mold, or molds, bearing in mind that the larger the mold the thicker the chocolate case should be (see step 4).

2 Make sure the mold is completely clean and dry, then spoon in some chocolate. Tip and rotate the mold so the chocolate flows to coat the sides completely and evenly.

3 Pour the excess chocolate back into the bulk of the chocolate, then leave the mold upside down on waxed paper to dry.

4 If the mold is large, apply a second, even a third layer, once the first one has set, to build up the right degree of thickness.

5 When the chocolate is hard, carefully remove any excess chocolate from the edges with a razor blade or sharp knife.

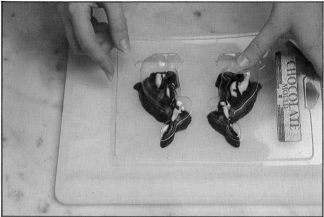

6 Gently tap the molds to release the cases of set chocolate.

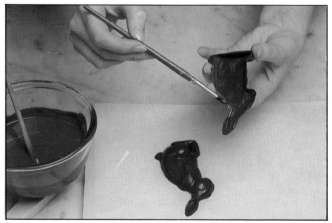

7 Spread a thin layer of melted chocolate over the rim of one of the cases, holding it steady on waxed paper. Place the second case on the first, again using waxed paper to shield the chocolate from the hands. Gently press the two halves together.

8 Decorate the outside with piped chocolate, crystalized flowers etc.

P·R·E·P·A·R·I·N·G N·U·T·S

Nuts for sweets must be perfectly dry, and when used for nougat or praline, they should be warmed slightly in a low oven so that they do not cause localized cooling and crystalization of the syrup. It is important also to prepare nuts properly before use. In particular, the fine skin that fits closely around each nut must be removed.

• ALMONDS •

1 Pour boiling water over the nuts, leave for a minute, then pour the water off.

• HAZELS AND BRAZILS •

1 Skins are easy to remove if the nuts are spread out on a baking tray and placed in an oven pre-heated to 325°F for 10 minutes.
2 Place the nuts in a colander and rub them with a cloth – the skins should flake off and fall through the holes.

2 It should then be easy to 'pop' the nuts out of the skins, while they are still warm.

3 If the skins remain firmly in place or if they cool, repeat the steeping process.

CRYSTALIZED CONFECTIONS

Crystalizing is the sweet-lover's favorite method of preserving a variety of suitable fruits, flowers, and fruit rinds, using a number of different techniques. Crystalized confections must be kept dry so pack them in an airtight container between layers of waxed paper and keep in a cool place.

• FRUITS •

The crystalizing of fruits is a lengthy process that must be done gradually over a number of days – about 14 – yet it is very simple to do. The results of your own crystalizing can be delicious as well as immensely satisfying, especially if you use fruits or flowers from your garden.

Fruits for crystalizing should be ripe, but firm, in perfect condition and free of blemishes. Small fruits such as cherries, apricots and plums can be left whole but should be pricked all over with a needle to allow the syrup to penetrate. Larger fruits such as a pineapple or peaches, which are peeled and cut into pieces, do not need to be pricked. Soft fruits such as raspberries and strawberries are unsuitable as they disintegrate.

Glacé fruits are crystalized fruits that have been dipped in a syrup to give them a glossy finish.

• FLOWERS •

The crystalizing process for flowers is much quicker than that for fruits but the initial preparation can be time-consuming as the entire surface of each petal must be painted evenly with gum arabic (available from chemists).

Small flowers such as violets and rose geraniums can be left whole, but larger ones, of which roses are the most popular example, are divided into petals. They must be in good condition, fresh and perfectly dry.

• FRUIT RINDS •

Rinds, from citrus fruits, are parboiled before being crystalized by simmering in a syrup to avoid a bitter taint to the finished sweet.

• CRYSTALIZING FRUITS •

1 Prepare the chosen fruit, then poach until just tender.

2 Transfer the fruit to a wire rack placed over a shallow tray and leave to drain.

3 Pour a syrup, made from 1¼ cups of the poaching liquor and ¾ cup sugar, over the fruit that has been placed in a shallow tray.

4 Using a fish slice, transfer the fruit to a wire rack, placed over a shallow tray.

5 Increase the concentration of the syrup by dissolving a further ¼ cup of sugar in it.

· CRYSTALIZING FLOWERS ·

1 Using a soft paint brush, coat flower petals with a mixture of gum arabic, rose water and food coloring.

2 Sift superfine sugar over the petals and leave on a wire rack in a warm place until dry and brittle.

M·A·R·Z·I·P·A·N

Homemade marzipan is an amenable chameleon amongst candies. It can be rolled, molded, cut and teased into a cornucopia of shapes from mushrooms to checkerboards. At the drop of a liquid food color it can be transformed into a rainbow of hues and tints.

· MARZIPAN CHECKERBOARD ·

1 Roll out each piece of marzipan separately on a work surface lightly sprinkled with confectioner's sugar to a rectangle about ¼ inch thick.

2 Brush one piece with lightly beaten egg white.

3 Lay the second piece on top and pass a rolling pin lightly over the top to gently press the pieces together.

4 After trimming the edges of the rectangle with a sharp knife, cut it lengthwise into 3 strips of equal width.

5 brush the top of one strip lightly with lightly beaten egg white.

6 Place another strip on top, making sure that it is completely lined up. Repeat with the remaining strip.

7 Cut the stack lengthwise into 4 strips with a long, sharp knife.

8 Lay one strip flat and place a second strip on the first, turning it over so the colors are reversed. Brush with egg white and repeat with the remaining strips, making sure the colors always alternate.

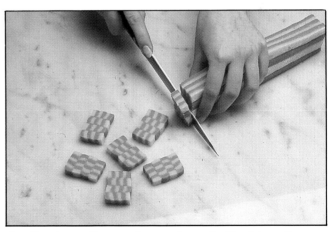

9 Cut into slices using a sharp knife then allow to dry on waxed paper for a few hours.

S·I·M·P·L·E C·A·N·D·I·E·S

There are many delicious candies that do not fall into the traditional categories, do not need any cooking, and can be made in a matter of moments. These are ideal for inexperienced cooks of all ages, and will easily get them into the swing of candy making. Alternatively, if you are short on time or need to provide candies in a hurry, any one of these simple goodies will serve you well.

C·O·C·O·N·U·T I·C·E
(uncooked)

MAKES ABOUT 1½ lb
•
⅔ cup condensed milk
•
good rounded cup confectioner's sugar, sifted
•
¾ cup shredded coconut
•
A few drops of pink food coloring

1 Dust a jelly roll pan or a square pan with extra confectioner's sugar.
2 Mix the condensed milk, confectioner's sugar and coconut together in a large bowl to give a fairly stiff mixture.
3 Divide in half, and add a few drops of food coloring to one half to give a delicate pink.
4 If using a rectangular pan, spread one mixture in one half, the other mixture in the other half, and press down firmly. If using a square pan, about 7 in, press one mixture over the base and press down firmly, then spread the other mixture over the top and press down firmly.
5 Leave to set, then cut into fingers or cubes with a lightly oiled knife.
6 Wrap in waxed paper and store in an airtight container in a cool place.

C·H·E·S·T·N·U·T C·R·A·C·K·L·E·S

MAKES ABOUT 30
•
10 oz-can unsweetened chestnuts, drained
•
1¼ cups milk
•
3 oz sponge cake, rubbed through a strainer
•
¼ cup superfine sugar
•
1 tablespoon brandy
•
1 tablespoon heavy cream
•
1 cup sugar

1 Gently cook the chestnuts in the milk for 10 minutes.
2 Strain into a bowl and beat in the crumbed sponge cakes, the ¼ cup superfine sugar, brandy and cream.
3 With wetted fingers form into small balls.
4 Leave on silicone paper to allow a skin to form.
5 Gently heat the 1 cup sugar in a heavy saucepan, shaking it occasionally, until the sugar has dissolved.
6 Increase the heat to 320–350°F and cook until it becomes a medium caramel color.
7 Remove from the heat and tilt the pan to form a pool of caramel, then lower in one chestnut ball at a time on a lightly oiled chocolate dipping fork, carving fork, or ordinary fork.
8 Place in small paper candy cases. Serve within a few hours.

• ABOVE •
Coconut Ice (top)
Chestnut Crackles (bottom)

27

• ABOVE •
Chocolate Nut Fudge
• OPPOSITE •
Praline Chocolate Layers

P·R·A·L·I·N·E CHOCOLATE L·A·Y·E·R·S

MAKES ABOUT 50–60

•

8 oz hazelnuts, lightly toasted

•

4 oz superfine sugar

•

1 tablespoon oil

•

1 lb dark chocolate

•

8 oz white chocolate, chopped

•

1½ tablespoons Kirsch

•

1 tablespoon Grand Marnier

1 Mix the nuts, sugar and oil together in a food processor or blender using on/off bursts until the mixture becomes an oily paste redolent of peanut butter. Scrape the bowl or goblet frequently.

2 Chop half the dark chocolate and melt it and the white chocolate separately in bowls placed over saucepans of hot water until their temperatures reach 110°F.

3 Beat half of the nut paste into each bowl of chocolate.

4 Add the Kirsch to the dark chocolate, the Grand Marnier to the white chocolate.

5 Divide each mixture in half and roll each piece out separately between 2 sheets of plastic wrap to a large rectangle. Turn the sheets over halfway through so that both sides will be flat.

6 Chill for about 10 minutes to firm up.

7 Remove the plastic wrap and stack the layers alternately on top of each other. Trim the edges using a large sharp knife.

8 Cut into strips about 1½ in wide.

9 Grate the remaining dark chocolate and melt it in a bowl placed over a saucepan of hot water.

10 Spread the strips with melted chocolate, working in one direction only.

11 Leave on waxed paper to set then cut into pieces with an oiled knife. Store in an airtight container in a cool place.

C·H·O·C·O·L·A·T·E N·U·T F·U·D·G·E

MAKES ABOUT 1¾ lb

•

2 oz dark unsweetened chocolate, chopped

•

scant 1 cup soft cheese

•

1 tablespoon light cream

•

1½ lb confectioner's sugar, sifted

•

¾ cup chopped nuts

•

A few drops of vanilla extract

1 Oil a pan approximately 7 in square.

2 Melt the chocolate in a bowl placed over a pan of hot water.

3 Beat the cheese with the cream until smooth.

4 Work the confectioner's sugar into the cream and cheese mixture, then beat in the chocolate.

5 Stir in the nuts and vanilla extract, then pour into the pan.

6 Press down firmly, cover and chill until almost set.

7 Mark into squares with a sharp knife and chill for several hours.

8 Keep in an airtight container in the refrigerator for up to 3 days.

C·O·F·F·E·E A·N·D W·A·L·N·U·T C·R·E·A·M·S

MAKES ABOUT 12 oz

•

3 heaped tablespoons full fat soft cheese

•

Approximately 2 teaspoons good quality coffee extract

•

Approximately 1⅓ cups sifted confectioner's sugar

•

2 oz dark chocolate, chopped

•

Walnut halves

1 Beat the cheese until smooth then beat in the coffee extract. Gradually beat in sufficient confectioner's sugar to give a stiff consistency.

2 Form the mixture into a smooth ball, then roll out on a surface lightly dusted with extra confectioner's sugar, using a rolling pin similarly dusted with confectioner's sugar, to ¼–½ in thick.

3 Cut into 1 in circles with a cutter dusted with confectioner's sugar. Allow to dry.

4 Melt the chocolate in a small bowl placed over a saucepan of hot water.

5 Place on a small teaspoon of chocolate on the top of each coffee cream. Press a walnut half on the chocolate while it is still soft, then allow to set.

C·H·O·C·O·L·A·T·E P·E·P·P·E·R·M·I·N·T C·R·E·A·M·S

(uncooked)

MAKES ABOUT 8 oz

•

1 egg white

•

Peppermint oil

•

1⅔ cup confectioner's sugar

•

4 oz dark chocolate, chopped

1 Lightly dust a work surface, rolling pin and a ½ in cutter with extra confectioner's sugar.

2 Whisk the egg white until it is foamy.

3 Add about 4 drops of peppermint oil.

4 Mix in sufficient confectioner's sugar to give a stiff but pliable paste.

5 Turn onto the work surface and knead until it is smooth and free of cracks.

6 Roll out to about ¼ in thick.

7 Cut into circles with a cutter.

8 Melt the chocolate in a bowl placed over a saucepan of hot water.

9 Using a skewer to spear the candies, dip them into the chocolate to coat them, allowing excess chocolate to drain back into the bowl. Keep the chocolate at the right temperature and consistency by removing or returning it from or to the heat as necessary.

10 Leave the candies on a wire rack to set.

P·E·A·N·U·T B·U·T·T·E·R C·R·E·A·M·S

MAKES ABOUT 15 oz

•

⅓ cup full fat soft cheese

•

Approximately 1¾ cups sifted confectioner's sugar

•

3 tablespoons smooth peanut butter

•

scant 1 tablespoon unsalted butter

•

A few drops of vanilla extract

•

Approximately 1½ oz unsalted peanuts, finely chopped

1 Beat the cheese until softened and smooth.

2 Gradually beat in the sugar, peanut butter, butter and vanilla extract to give a stiff consistency. If necessary add a little more confectioner's sugar.

3 Cover and chill the mixture for 1–2 hours.

4 Form into small balls and roll each ball in finely chopped peanuts.

5 Place in paper candy cases, cover and keep refrigerated for up to 4 days. Return to room temperature about 2 hours before eating.

• ABOVE •
Peanut Butter Creams (top)
Chocolate Peppermint Creams (center)
Coffee Walnut Creams (bottom)

T·R·U·F·F·L·E·S

Truffles combine simplicity with melting deliciousness. They are among the easiest and quickest of candies to make, yet can be the most mouthwatering, bringing true sophistication within the reach of even the most amateur of cooks.

There is a vast array of recipes for truffles. Chocolate is the common ingredient, but after that the choice is enormous: cream and liqueurs for dinner-party 'specials,' butter, nuts or fruits or ground almonds in the form of marzipan as a base. They can also be made more economically with fine cake crumbs.

Truffles usually benefit from being kept for a few hours before being eaten, but they should not be kept for more than about 3 days, which provides a wonderful excuse for you to be greedy and unrestrained!

C·A·R·O·B T·R·U·F·F·L·E·S

MAKES ABOUT 10
•
3 tablespoons unsweetened carob powder
•
1 tablespoon instant coffee powder
•
2 tablespoons clear honey
•
1 tablespoon unsalted butter, diced
•
2 tablespoons skimmed milk powder
•
Carob powder flavored with ground cinnamon, for coating

1 Mix the carob and coffee powders together in a bowl.

2 Add the honey, place over a saucepan of hot water and heat until evenly blended.
3 Remove from the heat and mix in the butter and milk powder.
4 Cool a little, then form into small balls. Roll lightly in carob powder flavored with ground cinnamon.
5 Place in small paper candy cases. Cover and leave in a cool place overnight before eating.

C·O·C·O·N·U·T T·R·U·F·F·L·E·S

MAKES ABOUT 12
•
2 oz dark chocolate, chopped
•
2 tablespoons light cream
•
¾ cup sifted confectioner's sugar
•
¼ cup shredded coconut
•
Grated dark or white chocolate, for coating

1 Heat the chocolate in a bowl placed over a saucepan of hot water until just melted.
2 Remove from the heat and beat in the cream.
3 Gradually work in the confectioner's sugar then the coconut.
4 Cover and chill until firm enough to handle.
5 Form into balls, coat in grated chocolate, and place in small candy cases.

• ABOVE •
*Coconut Truffles made with white and
dark chocolate*
• OPPOSITE •
Carob Truffles

33

C·H·O·C·O·L·A·T·E W·O·R·K

For most candy lovers, chocolates are the ultimate in confections. Fondants are fine, as are crystalized fruits, marzipans and caramels, but give them a dark, glossy coating and they become sublime, an indulgence impossible to ignore.

C·H·O·C·O·L·A·T·E C·O·A·T·E·D F·R·U·I·T·S A·N·D N·U·T·S

1 Drop the items to be coated individually into the melted chocolate, turn them over with a dipping fork, or ordinary fork, then lift out.

2 Tap the fork on the side of the bowl, then draw the underside of the fork across the rim of the bowl.
3 Carefully transfer the coated item to waxed paper and set aside to dry.
4 Place in small paper candy cases, place in a single layer in a gift box and keep in a cool place.

• CHOCOLATE COATED MARZIPAN AND FONDANT •

1 Form the marzipan or fondant into the shapes required then allow to dry for 24 hours.
2 Drop the items to be coated individually into the melted chocolate, turn them over with a dipping fork, or ordinary fork, then lift out.
3 Tap the fork on the side of the bowl, then draw the underside of the fork across the rim of the bowl.
4 Carefully transfer the coated item to waxed paper and allow to dry.
5 Place in small paper candy cases, place in a single layer in a gift box and keep in a cool place.

• ABOVE •
Chocolate Coated Marzipan and Fondants
• OPPOSITE •
Chocolate Coated Fruit and Nuts

J·E·L·L·I·E·D F·R·U·I·T
C·A·N·D·I·E·S

The diversity of jellied candies ranges from the sparkling simplicity of fruit jellies to the sophistication of crème de menthe, from the Eastern promise of Turkish delight, to cloud-like marshmallows. Jellied candies can be cut into simple shapes after setting using a knife that has been wetted to prevent it sticking, or into more fancy shapes with wetted small cutters, or the liquid jelly can be poured on to a wetted fondant mat before being left to set to make jellies with a professional look.

F·R·U·I·T J·E·L·L·I·E·S

MAKES 1 lb
•
1 oz gelatin
•
1¼ cups clear fruit juice (eg, lemon, orange, blackcurrant, strawberry, raspberry), strained if necessary
•
⅓ cup sugar
•
4 tablespoons liquid glucose
•
Food coloring (optional)
•
Superfine sugar (optional)

1 Wet a pan approximately 6 in square.
2 Soften the gelatin in 4 tablespoons water.
3 Gently heat the fruit juice, sugar, and glucose in a heavy saucepan until the sugar has dissolved, stirring with a wooden spoon.
4 Stir in the gelatin and continue to heat gently, stirring, until the gelatin has dissolved.
5 If the liquid is too pale add a few drops of appropriate food coloring.
6 Pour into the pan and allow to set in a cool place for at least 6 hours.
7 Turn the jelly out of the pan onto a cold work surface and cut into squares or shapes with a sharp knife or cutter.
8 Serve plain or roll in superfine sugar.
9 Sugar-coated jellies can be kept in a cool place in an airtight container for a few days.

O·R·A·N·G·E S·L·I·C·E·S

MAKES ABOUT 8 oz
•
¾ cup sugar
•
6 tablespoons powdered glucose
•
1 oz powdered gelatin
•
⅔ cup strained fresh orange juice
•
Superfine sugar, for coating

1 Wet a pan approximately 8 in square and a 1½ in round cutter.
2 Mix the sugar, glucose, and gelatin together in a heavy saucepan.
3 Stir in the orange juice using a wooden spoon.
4 Heat gently, stirring, until the sugar and gelatin have dissolved.
5 Pour into the wet pan and allow to set.
6 Dip the bottom of the pan briefly in hot water and turn the jelly out.
7 Cut into crescent shapes using the wet cutter.
8 Roll the jellies in superfine sugar to coat them evenly.
9 Store in an airtight container lined with waxed paper. Separate layers with waxed paper.

• LEMON SLICES •
Use ⅔ cup strained fresh lemon juice instead of orange juice.

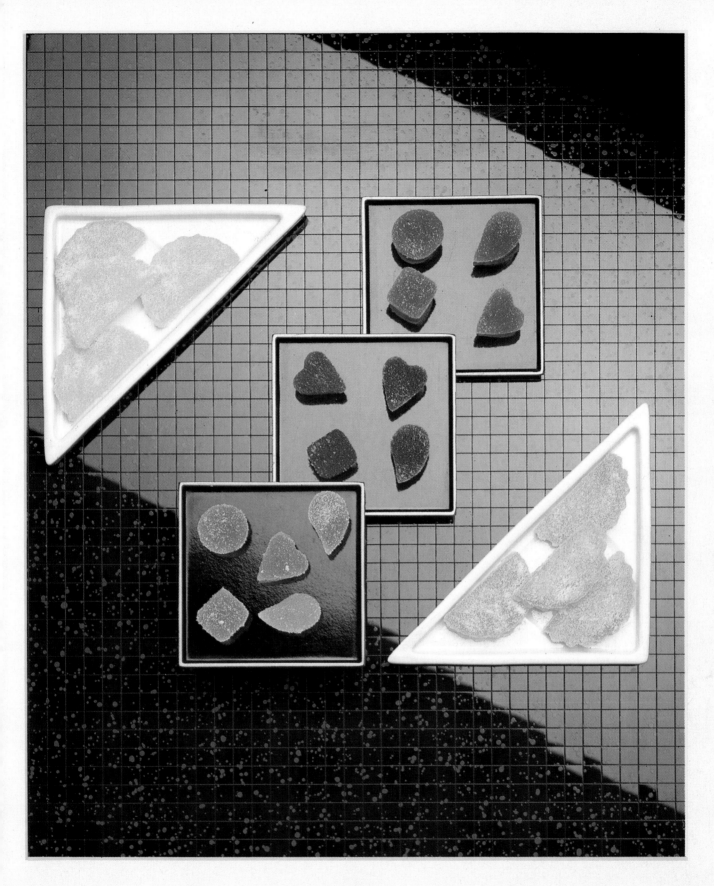

• ABOVE •
Lemon Slices (top)
Fruit Jellies (center)
Orange Slices (bottom)

37

• ABOVE •
Turkish Delight

T·U·R·K·I·S·H D·E·L·I·G·H·T

(traditional method)

MAKES ABOUT 1½ lb

·

1 lb sugar

·

¼ teaspoon tartaric acid

·

9 tablespoons cornstarch

·

1⅓ cups sifted confectioner's sugar

·

¼ cup clear honey

·

A few drops of lemon extract

·

A few drops of rose water

·

Red food coloring

·

For the coating

·

Approximately 1⅓ cups sifted confectioner's sugar

1 Butter or oil a pan approximately 12 × 4 in.
2 Gently heat the sugar in ¼ pt water in a heavy saucepan, stirring with a wooden spoon, until the sugar has dissolved.
3 Bring to a boil, cover and boil for 3 minutes.
4 Uncover and boil until the temperature reaches 240°F, the soft ball stage.
5 Add the tartaric acid and remove from the heat.
6 Blend the cornstarch and confectioner's sugar with ⅔ cup water in a heavy saucepan.
7 Bring 2½ cups water to a boil, then stir into the cornstarch/sugar paste. Bring to a boil, stirring, and beat vigorously until thick and opaque.
8 Lower the heat and gradually beat in the sugar syrup. Boil for 30 minutes until the mixture is a very pale straw color and transparent.
9 Beat in the honey, lemon extract, and rose water.
10 Pour half of the mixture into the pan. Add sufficient red food coloring to the remaining mixture to color it pale pink, then pour onto the mixture in the pan.
11 Put aside until cold and set.
12 Cut into squares with a sharp knife dipped in confectioner's sugar. Toss the pieces in confectioner's sugar.

T·U·R·K·I·S·H D·E·L·I·G·H·T

(quick method)

MAKES ABOUT 1¼ lb

·

2 oz gelatin

·

1 lb sugar

·

¼ teaspoon citric acid

·

Rose water

·

Red food coloring

·

Bare ½ cup sugar

·

3 tablespoons cornstarch

1 Pour ½ pt water into a heavy saucepan, sprinkle the gelatin over it, and leave to soften for 5 minutes.
2 Stir in the sugar and citric acid and heat gently until the sugar has dissolved, stirring with a wooden spoon.
3 Boil until the temperature reaches 240°F, soft ball stage.
4 Remove from the heat and leave to stand for 10 minutes.
5 Add the rose water to taste.
6 Pour half of the mixture into a pan approximately 8 × 6 in. Add a few drops of food coloring to the remaining mixture, then pour that over the first mixture.
7 Leave in a cool place for 24 hours.
8 Sift the confectioner's sugar and cornstarch together, then sprinkle evenly over a sheet of waxed paper.
9 Turn the Turkish delight onto the paper and cut into squares with a sharp knife.
10 Toss the squares in the sugar mixture to coat them evenly.
11 Store in an airtight container between layers of waxed paper and keep in a cool place.

M·A·R·S·H·M·A·L·L·O·W·S

MAKES ABOUT 1lb
•
1 lb sugar
•
1 tablespoon liquid glucose
•
1 oz powdered gelatin
•
2 tablespoons orange flower water
•
2 egg whites
•
*Cornstarch and sifted confectioner's sugar,
for dusting and coating*

1 Lightly oil a pan approximately 8 in square and dust it with a mixture of equal quantities of cornstarch and sifted confectioner's sugar.

2 Gently heat the sugar with the glucose and 7 fl oz water in a heavy saucepan, stirring with a wooden spoon, until the sugar has dissolved.

3 Bring to a boil, cover and boil for 3 minutes.

4 Uncover and boil until the temperature reaches 260°F, the hard ball stage.

5 Meanwhile, dissolve the gelatin in ½ cup water in a bowl placed over a saucepan of hot water.

6 Pour the gelatin into the syrup and add the orange flower water.

7 Whisk the egg whites until stiff.

8 Pour the syrup into the egg whites in a slow, thin, steady stream, whisking constantly.

9 Whisk until the mixture is thick and stiff.

10 Spread the mixture in the pan, using a spatula to smooth it out evenly, and leave to set.

11 Spread a work surface with cornstarch/ confectioner's sugar mixture.

12 Run a small knife around the edges of the pan to loosen the mixture, then turn it out onto the surface.

13 Dust the top and sides with more cornstarch/ confectioner's sugar mixture to coat them evenly.

14 Cut into circles using an oiled 1 in cutter, or into squares by cutting first into 1 in wide strips using an oiled large, sharp knife, then oiled scissors to form the squares.

15 Coat the sides of the shapes in cornstarch/confectioner's sugar mixture and leave to dry on a wire rack for 24 hours.

16 Store in an airtight container lined with waxed paper. Separate layers of marshmallows with waxed paper.

• ROSE MARSHMALLOWS •
Use rose water instead of orange flower water and add a few drops of pink food coloring, if liked.

• LEMON MARSHMALLOWS •
Use a few drops of lemon oil instead of orange flower water and add a few drops of yellow food coloring, if liked.

• PEPPERMINT MARSHMALLOWS •
Add a few drops of peppermint oil instead of orange flower water and add a few drops of green food coloring, if liked.

• COCONUT MARSHMALLOWS •
Coat the candies in shredded coconut instead of the cornstarch/confectioner's sugar mixture.

D·I·V·I·N·I·T·Y

MAKES ABOUT 1lb
•
1⅓ cups sugar
•
5 tablespoons light corn syrup
•
1 teaspoon vinegar
•
1 egg white
•
A few drops vanilla extract
•
3 oz mixed nuts, chopped

1 Gently heat the sugar, syrup and vinegar with ½ cup water in a heavy saucepan, stirring with a wooden spoon, until the sugar has dissolved and the syrup melted.

2 Bring to a boil, cover and cook for 3 minutes.

3 Uncover and boil until the temperature reaches 250°F, the hard ball stage.

4 Meanwhile whisk the egg white in a large bowl, set over a pan of just-simmering water, until it holds its shape.

5 Slowly pour the syrup into the egg white in a thin, steady stream, whisking constantly.

6 Stir in the vanilla extract and the nuts.

7 Beat until the mixture will hold its shape then drop small balls onto waxed paper.

8 Store in an airtight container and eat soon after making.

• ABOVE •
Marshmallows (top)
Divinity (bottom)

R·U·M A·N·D R·A·I·S·I·N F·U·D·G·E

MAKES ABOUT 1lb

•

Scant 1 cup demerara sugar

Scant 1 cup superfine sugar

4 tablespoons unsalted butter, diced

⅔ cup light cream

1 tablespoon dark rum

⅓ cup seedless raisins

1 Butter or oil a pan approximately 9 in square.
2 Gently heat the sugars, butter and cream in a heavy saucepan until the sugars have dissolved and the butter melted, stirring with a wooden spoon.

3 Add the rum and bring to a boil. Cover and boil for 3 minutes.
4 Uncover and boil until the temperature reaches 240°F, the soft ball stage.
5 Plunge the bottom of the saucepan immediately into cold water.
6 Cool for 5 minutes, then beat vigorously with a wooden spoon until the mixture is thick, creamy and pale in color.
7 Stir in the raisins.
8 Pour into the pan and leave until almost cold.
9 Mark into squares with a lightly oiled knife and leave until firm.
10 Cut into pieces and store in a cool place in an airtight container between layers of waxed paper.

O·P·E·R·A F·U·D·G·E

MAKES ABOUT 1lb

•

1¾ cups sugar

•

1 cup heavy cream

•

A few drops of vanilla extract

1 Oil a pan approximately 8 in square.
2 Gently heat the sugar and cream in a heavy saucepan, stirring with a wooden spoon, until the sugar has dissolved.
3 Bring to a boil, cover and boil for 3 minutes.
4 Uncover and boil until the temperature reaches 234°F, the soft ball stage.
5 Dip the bottom of the saucepan in cold water and leave to cool to 110°F.
6 Add the vanilla extract and beat until the mixture becomes thick and creamy in color.
7 Pour into the pan, cover with a damp cloth and leave for 30 minutes.
8 Uncover and leave until just set. Mark into squares with a lightly oiled knife and allow to set completely.
9 Cut or break into pieces and store in an airtight container between layers of waxed paper.

• ABOVE •
Opera Fudge
• OPPOSITE •
Rum and Raisin Fudge

• ABOVE •
Checkerboard (top right)
Harlequin Marzipan (top left)
Neapolitan Slices (bottom left)
• OPPOSITE •
Neapolitan Slices

44

S·O·P·H·I·S·T·I·C·A·T·E·D I·D·E·A·S U·S·I·N·G M·A·R·Z·I·P·A·N

• MARZIPAN CHECKERBOARD •

1 Divide a piece of marzipan in half and knead a few drops of food coloring into one piece.

2 Roll out each piece separately on a work surface lightly sprinkled with confectioner's sugar to a rectangle about ¼ in thick.

3 Brush one piece with lightly beaten egg white, then lay the second piece on top. Pass a rolling pin lightly over the top to gently press the pieces together.

4 Trim the edges of the rectangle with a sharp knife then cut it lengthwise into 3 strips of equal width.

5 Brush the top of one strip lightly with lightly beaten egg white and place another strip on top, making sure that it is completely lined up. Repeat with the remaining strip.

6 Pass a rolling pin over the stack to press the pieces together.

7 With a long, sharp knife cut the stack lengthwise into 4 strips.

8 Lay one strip flat, brush with egg white and place a second strip on the first, turning it over so the colors are reversed. Brush with egg white and repeat with the remaining strips, making sure the colors always alternate.

9 Pass the rolling pin lightly over the stack.

10 Cut into slices using a sharp knife then leave to dry on waxed paper for a few hours.

• HARLEQUIN MARZIPAN •

1 Color 3 or 4 pieces of marzipan, all the same size, with a few drops of contrasting food colors.

2 On a surface lightly dusted with confectioner's sugar roll each piece out separately to rectangles of the same size about ¼ in thick.

3 Brush the top of one piece lightly with lightly beaten egg white, lay another on top and pass the rolling pin lightly over to press them together gently.

4 Brush the top lightly with egg white and repeat with the remaining pieces.

5 Trim the edges using a large, sharp knife then cut into pieces.

6 Coat the pieces in superfine sugar, pressing it in gently, then leave for several hours to dry.

• NEAPOLITAN MARZIPAN SLICES •

1 Knead a few drops of 2 contrasting food colorings – red and green, for instance – into 2 equal sized pieces of marzipan.

2 Color a third piece of the same size yellow.

3 On a surface lightly dusted with confectioner's sugar roll the 2 colored pieces of marzipan separately into strips ½ inch thick and about 1 in wide.

4 Cut each strip in half lengthwise using a sharp knife and trim them so all the pieces are exactly the same size.

5 Roll the yellow piece of marzipan out very thinly to the same length as the strips and about 4½in wide. Brush with lightly beaten egg white.

6 Place 2 strips of different colors along the plain strip, brush the tops with beaten egg white, then place the other 2 strips on top of them so the colors are reversed.

7 Wrap the plain marzipan around the strips to resemble a Battenburg cake, gently pressing all the pieces of marzipan together.

8 Cut into slices using a sharp knife.

L·O·L·L·I·P·O·P·S

1 lb sugar

•

1 tablespoon powdered glucose

•

*3 or 4 flavorings and appropriate food colorings
(eg, orange oil and orange coloring, raspberry
flavoring and red coloring, lemon oil and yellow
coloring, peppermint oil and green coloring)*

•

Lollipop sticks

1 Oil a marble surface or large baking sheet.
2 Gently heat the sugar and glucose in ⅔ cup water in a heavy saucepan, stirring with a wooden spoon, until the sugar has dissolved.
3 Pour into a measuring jug and measure off one-third or one-quarter, depending on whether 3 or 4 flavorings are being used.
4 Add the chosen coloring to the measured-off amount, bring to a boil, cover and boil for 3 minutes.
5 Uncover and boil until the temperature reaches 265°F, the hard ball stage. Remove from the heat and add the appropriate flavoring.
6 Drop small, round pools of the syrup onto the oiled surface using a dessert or soup spoon. Lay a lollipop stick in each pool. Add a little more syrup, if necessary, to cover the sticks.
7 Leave to harden then carefully remove from the surface and wrap individually in cellophane paper.
8 Repeat with the remaining syrup in batches, using different colorings and flavorings.

B·A·R·L·E·Y S·U·G·A·R T·W·I·S·T·S

MAKES ABOUT 1lb

•

2 tablespoons pearl barley

•

Thinly pared zest and juice of ½ lemon

•

1 lb sugar

•

¼ teaspoon cream of tartar

1 Put the barley into a saucepan. Stir in ½ pt cold water and bring to a boil.
2 Drain the barley and rinse it under cold running water.
3 Return the barley to the rinsed saucepan, stir in 3¾ cups cold water and the lemon zest. Bring to a boil, reduce the heat, cover and simmer for about 1½–1¾ hours until the barley is soft.
4 Strain off the liquid, add the lemon juice and make up to 2½ cups with cold water.
5 Lightly oil a marble surface or baking sheet.
6 Gently heat the sugar, cream of tartar and barley water in a heavy saucepan, stirring constantly with a wooden spoon, until the sugar has dissolved.
7 Bring to a boil, cover and boil for 3 minutes.
8 Uncover and boil until the temperature reaches 310°F, the hard crack stage.
9 Pour the syrup onto the surface or baking sheet so that it spreads out to an even shallow pool.
10 Leave the barley sugar to cool until it firms around the edges.
11 Using a lightly oiled metal spatula, ease one edge of the sheet of syrup away from the surface or baking sheet, then pull the edge up with your hands and fold it over the middle of the sheet of syrup, laying it down evenly so that there are no wrinkles.
12 Immediately fold the opposite edge over to meet the first edge in the middle.
13 Gently lift the folded sheet using the oiled spatula and, cutting alternately from opposite sides of the sheet, cut it into strips about ½ in wide with oiled scissors. Twist each strip into a spiral as it is cut.
14 Leave the strips to harden then wrap individually in cellophane and store in an airtight container.

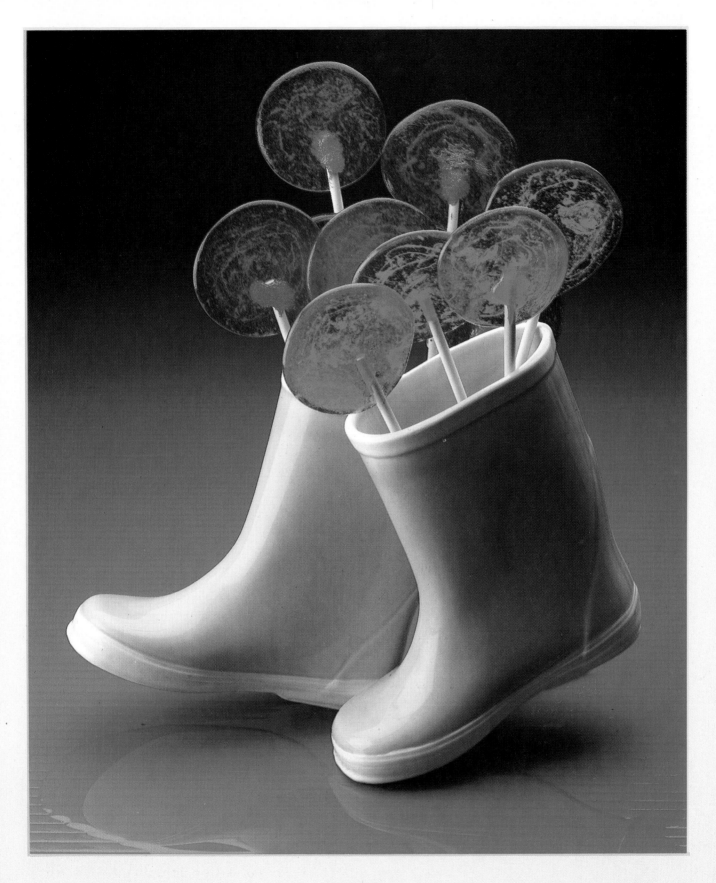

• ABOVE •
Lollipops
• OPPOSITE •
Barley Sugar Twists

R·O·S·E C·R·E·A·M·S

MAKES ABOUT 8 oz

•

5 teaspoons lemon juice

•

½ teaspoon finely grated lemon zest

•

4 teaspoons rosehip syrup

•

A few drops of rose water

•

8 oz confectioner's sugar, sifted

•

Crystalized rose petals, for decoration

1 Mix the lemon juice, lemon zest, rosehip syrup and rose water together.

2 Add the confectioner's sugar and work to a stiff mixture using the fingertips.

3 Break off small pieces of the mixture and roll into balls on a work surface lightly dusted with extra sifted confectioner's sugar.

4 Flatten each ball slightly and place a piece of crystalized rose petal on top. Press lightly in place.

5 Place the creams in small paper candy cases and leave in a cool place to dry.

V·I·O·L·E·T C·R·E·A·M·S

MAKES ABOUT 8 oz

•

A few drops of violet extract

•

A few drops of violet food coloring

•

8 oz fondant (any variety)

•

Crystalized violets, for decoration

1 Knead the extract and food coloring into the fondant and leave for 1 hour.

2 Shape into small balls and flatten each one lightly.

3 Place a small piece of crystalized violet in the center of each.

4 Leave to dry for 24 hours.

C·O·C·O·N·U·T A·N·D L·E·M·O·N C·R·E·A·M·S

MAKES ABOUT 12 oz

•

Confectioner's sugar, for dusting

•

A few drops of lemon oil

•

½ cup shredded coconut

•

8 oz fondant (any variety)

•

A few drops of pink food coloring

•

Superfine sugar, for coating

1 On a surface lightly dusted with confectioner's sugar, knead the lemon oil and coconut into the fondant.

2 Divide the mixture in half and work a little pink food coloring into one half.

3 Using a rolling pin lightly dusted with confectioner's sugar roll each piece into a strip about ¼ in thick.

4 Place the pink strip on top of the white one and press the two together lightly with a rolling pin.

5 Sprinkle with superfine sugar and leave for 24 hours to dry.

6 Cut into small bars with a sharp knife, and store in a single layer in an airtight container lined with waxed paper, and covered with waxed paper.